Take a Leap of

Faith

And Start a

Virtual Assistant

Business

Your Guide to Establishing a Successful Business

As a Virtual Assistant

Russell Davis

Table of Contents

Introduction

A virtual assistant is the extension of the client. What the client cannot do, he will perform. Hence, it is important to underline a fact that is often missed by many: <u>being a virtual assistant is NOT easy</u>. Just because you stay at home doesn't mean your job is cozy.

So, why are people getting crazy over the idea of starting a virtual assistant business? First, there's convenience of staying at home with your family. Second, you will become your own boss. Third, and perhaps the most appealing: the possibility to earn a lot of money is endless.

In this book, you will learn about the following:

- Qualifications of a VA

- Common niches

- Tips in setting up your office

- How to find your client, including tips in writing a pitch

- Business promotion

- Legalities of VA Business

- Getting paid

- What to do after the job

- What to do if you encounter nightmare clients.

- Furthering your business

- And many more!

As long as you are capable of working in front of a computer, you CAN be a virtual assistant. You just need to be well-equipped; hopefully, this book will help you.

Chapter 1 - Most Common Qualifications that Clients Look For in a Virtual Assistant

Let's face it: even though a virtual assistant generally works in front of a computer, clients still look for certain qualifications before hiring anyone; and why not? The job of a VA, after all, is *very* important in terms of keeping things working smoothly for the client. As we have mentioned earlier, being a virtual assistant means you become an extension of the person whom you are working for: he (or she) is so busy that delegation of tasks must be enforced.

Education

There is no need for you to have a college degree, UNLESS the job posted is highly technical; for example, a doctor who needs someone to "monitor" his patients via phone calls must hire someone who is knowledgeable in medications, signs and symptoms of diseases, and treatment. If he wants what's best for his clients, he would take a professional medical practitioner, like a nurse. But don't worry, most of VA jobs are simpler than that, so a high school diploma or a GED is often enough to start the business.

Experience

This is the part when things become tricky; if you'll scout online hiring websites, you will notice that most clients who look for a virtual assistant want to have someone who is already experienced. What if you are just starting out? Will they dismiss your proposal right away? No, they won't. The sad fact is they might hire you, but with a significantly lower rate than experienced assistants charge. Don't fall into that trap unless their rate is acceptable for you. You may not have the experience as a VA, but if your work is almost similar to the description given and the only difference is that you will now be performing it at home instead of in the office, then you can surely count that as experience. My advice, if you are inexperienced, is for you to take a Virtual Assistants Training Online.

Here's the deal: I will list down all the basic skills you need; if you find that you lack any of them, then DO NOT start your business yet. This is because all that I am about to enumerate are the foundations of being a VA – if you don't have them, chances are, you will only cause frustration on your client and he might flag you.

- **Organization Skills** – A client will hire you because he doesn't like mess, so if you will just ruin his schedule, lose his files, and "forget" deadlines, he would be much better off without you. You have to orient yourself with organizational tools, like Dropbox, Box, Azendoo, Asana, Trello, Evernote, and Google Docs.

- **Computer Skills** – Knowledge in MS Word, Excel, and PowerPoint, is important as well as knowing how to maintain and troubleshoot your PC. Your typing speed need not to be out-of-this-world, but it should also be competent

- **Internet Skills** – What do you know about E-mails? How accurate are you when you search some queries? Are you capable of handling social media accounts like Facebook, Twitter, Instagram, and Pinterest? Most of the clients want VAs for this purpose alone, so you better be prepared.

- **Communication Skills** – Are you comfortable in communicating with your client? Can you talk to him fluently in the language he is used to? How will you communicate? Most of the time, e-mails are enough, but if not, tools like Skype is required.

When we say "special" it means that not anyone can do what you can do – like the example we had earlier about a doctor who wants to monitor his patients via phone calls. Someone who has no medical training will have difficulty in identifying a covert distress call, but a medical student, a nurse, or a caregiver will be able to spot it with ease.

Another example is writing. Writing seems to be an easy enough job for anyone, but if the client wants his VA to write copies from time to time, it then becomes technical as not everyone has the skills of a copywriter.

If you have a special skill, then you might as well find VA jobs which involve them; use these skills to your advantage.

Chapter 2 - Setting Up Your Office

Even though you will be working from home, you still need a professional space, hence, I made this chapter. Setting up a home workspace is easy; let me rephrase that: setting up a home workspace is fun! First, you can choose whatever space you want, so long as it satisfies 2 criteria: a) it's quiet and b) it's comfortable. After that, you can pretty much follow the steps below:

1. Set up the "borders" – Having boundaries can go a long, long way – believe me. First, it helps if you have roommates: you can tell them right away that this space is a workplace, so they shouldn't mess with it. If you live alone, having borders means you can relax outside the station. And last but not the least, it will help you organize things. Once boundaries are established, you shouldn't let work-related files and paper stray outside.

2. List down what you need – Start out in an organized fashion by listing down the things that you need. From scraps of paper, to highlighters and calendars – put them in writing and keep the list because you might want to "restock" in the future. IMPORTANT: Avoid adding things that are not really necessary: for an instance, if you don't need your tablet PC beside you, don't place it in the office as it can only serve as a distraction.

3. Be inspired – Some people want to have inspirations plastered in the office; if you are one of them, don't hold back! Cut out pictures and post them on the wall or frame them up! This step is not luxury, it's essential to keep you going especially on days when things get rough. You can even get crafty while setting up your station!

4. The Proper Posture – Just because you will work from home doesn't mean you'll abandon proper posture. Don't. It may cause you pain and may hinder you from accomplishing tasks. Remember the following:

- Avoid buying a table where there is an underside space for the keyboard. Most virtual assistants think it's beneficial since it saves space, but the truth is, this feature is detrimental for your arms' health while typing or moving the mouse.

- Invest in a TFT monitor to prevent unnecessary tiring of the eyes; it also has no radiation danger, so you'll feel better using it.

- As for distance, position your face at an arm's length in front of the monitor. Adjust the font size of the browser and PC, so you'll be at ease.

- Choose a table with adequate space, so as you can keep frequently needed materials close by.

- Select a chair which height can be adjusted. If you like to relax in between work, buy one that has adjustable inclination. Remember that your knees should be slightly lower than your thigh to keep the blood flowing in your legs and feet.

5. Work on your budget – Don't overspend just to have a posh workspace. Most VAs make good money, so you can expect their station to be "state-of-the-art", but if you are just starting out, just use whatever budget you have to the best of your ability. Don't worry, as you continue to grow, your home office also will!

However you want your workspace to be, remember this: **you should be organized**. Try to have a big calendar to see your schedule right away and have post-its for your daily tasks.

Chapter 3 - Choose Your Own Niche

Almost every job has different niches under them: teachers fall into different subjects and levels, doctors have specialties, and writers could be bloggers or copywriters. Virtual assistants also have niches depending on what the client needs. I will list down some of the niches below, but please remember that it is not an exhaustive list. Other niches are available in the market and you have to be on the lookout for them especially if something related to your profession comes.

Bookkeeping – Are you in the financing sector? If yes, you will find that bookkeeping VAs are in demand! This is because businesses worldwide need someone to handle bills, payment to employees, invoicing of supplies, and other financial matters like taxes.

Real Estate – You may think that real estate agents can do things on their own, but the truth is, there are a lot of things happening behind selling houses and collecting mortgage payments. As a virtual assistant, you might work on marketing the house for sale, assisting in filing the documents, or maintaining the company's website.

Social Media – Social Media savvy? If yes, then here's the good news: business around the globe know that to be in the loop, they have to enter the social media hype. Not all owners are knowledgeable in that area, and most of them won't have the time, so they will opt to pass the job to someone else. Some of the tasks given to a social media VA are:

- Writing posts or tweets
- Finding content to share
- Answering queries from clients or customers

- Making sure that each post/content share will reach the people
- Creating ads or campaign

Author/Publisher – Nowadays, publishing a book has never been easy. You literally just have to research, write, and upload. Hence, authors worldwide want to concentrate on writing rather than busy themselves with things that other people can do for them. Working with an author or a publishing company ensures that you will be busy; some of the tasks included are:

- Researching on topics
- Formatting and uploading the book
- Maintaining the website
- Manage the author's social media accounts
- Giving free copies in exchange for honest reviews
- Beta-reading, proofreading, and editing

- Marketing the book

- Arranging the schedule of authors for book signing, interview, and talks.

Transcription – Transcription is a common job for legal and medical matters, but to date, anyone can use it for their own field. Transcribing podcasts, seminars, interviews, and talks can be made into e-books, audio books, or blog posts. As a VA, you need to incorporate some research to make it suitable for sharing.

Aside from these major niches, you can also choose to work for a person whose profession or business is expanding. Almost all kinds of expanding profession or business will require delegation and many of them would choose to work with a VA rather than hire someone personally because of the many benefits which we have discussed in the introduction.

Selecting a niche comes down to two things: a) what you already know, and b) what you want to do. If you want to stay in your line of profession, then good, because there will be a little need to re-orient yourself. However, if you plan to take a niche that is different from what you are familiar with, be ready to study and practice.

Think long and hard when deciding on the niche; it wouldn't do you any good to jump from one specialization to another because clients will look for your experience not as a VA in general, but as a VA in *their* field. Someone who has a 2-year experience as a real estate virtual assistant will definitely look better than a person with 6 months' experience in real estate, 8 months as a VA to an author, and 10 months as an assistant to an events specialist.

But what if I want to try my hand on several niches first so I will know exactly what I like? Will that look bad on my profile?

You can do that, too! But make sure you will look for clients who are looking for a short-term VA. And once you have signed a contract, make certain that you will do your best even if you realize that his niche is not yours.

Chapter 4 - Finding Your Client

One of the worst mistakes a VA business owner does is this: they see a VA position and readily apply for it. It's a syndrome, in my opinion. You become so eager to have a contract that you fail to "screen" your clients.

That's right, folks – YOU also have to see if the client will fit the criteria you are looking for; you are not an employee – you are a business owner, so don't think, even for a second, that only the client can make demands.

Below are some guidelines in finding clients:

Where to Look?

First concern: where do I find my clients? As a first-timer, your best choice is to start on popular online hiring platforms such as: Upwork, Freelancer, Guru, and Fiverr.

Upwork has the most number of clients, BUT it also has the most number of contractors, so expect competition to be tough. **Freelancer** is almost the same, but I find their fees a little confusing. Before, I hired someone there, and they charged me once for the project and another when my contractor accepted the terms. I don't know how much the fees are for contractors, so investigate first. **Guru** has less clients, but I like their system – the fees are straightforward. **Fiverr** is also a good site, but you will find that it's different. You create a service and let clients buy them from you starting at $5. If you want to try out different niches, Fiverr is good, but there's less VA posts.

All these sites allow you to build your profile, so again, when a contract is started, do your best. Once you have established a great reputation, start a website, promote it, and let clients come to you!

NOTE: You can also find VA job posts at Indeed.com or Craigslist.

What to Look for in a Client?

Now, as for the criteria we are talking about – below are some of the things you should look for in a client:

- **Job description** – The first thing you have to inspect is the job description; what is this client expecting from his future VA? Are you capable of handling the project? Is he expecting you to squeeze a lot of tasks in the schedule he mentioned? What about the pay? IMPORTANT: If you feel that the client is asking too much for a meager pay, stay away from him. Chances are, he is also scope creep – someone who will ask you to do things that are not originally in the description. Another thing: when you see in the job post that you are expected to perform "other tasks..." don't forget to elaborate them in the contract.

- **Feedback** – Contractors in well-known platforms have the ability to leave comments and feedback. Once you feel that the job suits you, go over the client's profile and read the reviews for him. You will be surprised at how some clients treat their contractors! While you are on it, see how much the client has spent – if he already spent hundreds or thousands, your chances of being scammed is minute.

- **His Google Standing** – Okay, it's not really his "Google" standing, but what will you find if you search his name? Most of the time, good quality clients will appear on Facebook and LinkedIn, AND the website of his business will appear. If your client "hides" his real name, consider it a red flag.

- **Mode of Communication** – I'll be honest with you; most high quality clients looking for VAs would require constant communication via tools like Skype or Google Hangouts, especially if the tasks require supervision or approval. It may sound hazy to not use the platform's message board, but that's really normal. Things that should alarm you are:

  1. When the client wants you to work right away without even having a contract drawn up. That means he didn't hire you! The online platforms we have mentioned above all have secured payment methods, in which case, funds should be available first before you start working. If the client asks you to start ASAP, decline – tell him you need a contract first, and the funds

should be secured in your chosen platform.

2. Some clients will *find* you using online platforms like Upwork, but they will *not* hire you there; be careful if this happens. First of all, there's an exclusivity clause in those platforms which says that once the client and contractor initiates a connection, the job MUST be managed right there. If the client says he'll pay you using other methods like wire transfer, PayPal, or Skrill, you will not be protected.

3. If the client didn't even bother to introduce himself, or if none of the documents presented to you bear his real name. Usernames are not legal, so stick with real name.

In the future, you may find it convenient to receive payment elsewhere, since your rates won't have deductions; it's okay **as long as you trust your client** and **there is a legal contract.**

Your Proposal or Bid

The main key to having a contract is a good proposal or bid, but I won't bore you with technicalities in this section. I'm going to tell you what clients (like myself) look for when they read your application:

- How likable you are;
- What are your skills and knowledge?

In other words, they are not looking for big words and appealing promises – they are looking for what you can offer them. To do that you must be straightforward with your proposal AND you have to get their attention. The following are the tips to do that:

- Make your first sentence standout by asking a question or writing the review from one of your clients.
- Give your qualifications, training, and experience IN CONNECTION to his niche.
- State the things he required you to include (rate, schedule, etc.)
- List down the things you know about the task he has in mind.

Again, you only need to prove that you are likable AND that you are an authority in his niche.

True or False: Working at Home as a Virtual Assistant needs no permit.

It's False.

As what had been reiterated earlier, VA's are business owners and because of that, they also need to secure all the necessary documents. It's different from one county to the next, so I will just cover the basics in this section:

- First of all, think of a suitable **business name**. Most virtual assistants use their name since they want to make a reputation; others create a witty username since this will represent them in various online hiring platforms.

- Go to your county's business information center and inquire about the **documents** you'll need: licensing, permits, zoning, and taxation. These packages are typically free and easy to acquire.

- What's your **business entity**? VAs typically start in a sole proprietorship structure where only one person manages the business and where there is no legal distinction between business and owner. Do you have a partner? Do you intend to legally separate yourself from your business (LLC)?

When in doubt, consult a lawyer. Your business entity will play a huge role on how you should run your business, so don't take it lightly.

Your Rates

Finally, we have now come to the discussion of the rates. As a virtual assistant, you can charge in two ways: a) per hour, and b) per project or assignment.

If you charge **per hour**, you must remember the following:

- The contract should specifically tell you when your working days are, what time to start, and what time to end. Example: Mondays – Fridays, 8:00 am to 4:00 pm. Protect yourself by stating that the client cannot ask you to complete a task outside of your working hours – that means he CANNOT send you documents to read in advance, ask you to send e-mails, or suggest that you call someone out of the 8-4-time frame. Also include break times and vacation privileges if you decide to have any.

- Another option is to charge higher if the client is asking you to work after the specified time frame. Hence, if your rate is $17 per hour, charge $20 for each hour you work in excess.

- Don't forget to ask an increase over time; possibly after a few months or so. This is because working at an hourly structure ensures that you become quicker and better at doing your job, that, after some time, you'll be able to accomplish more in less time. If you notice that your client is already adding more tasks, it's time to increase your rate.

- Take into consideration the fact that no company is backing you up now. You will have no paid sick leave, no paid vacation time, you are basically paying for all your supplies, and the electricity and phone you are using are no longer company-owned.

The following statement is just my opinion: if you are starting out, charge your clients per hour. That way, you will be able to familiarize yourself with the twists and turns of your niche. After getting quicker and better, you can start charging **per**

project, in which case you need to keep the following in mind:

- Basically, you'll be incorporating your hourly rate here, but this time, you'll be able to have some leverage – you can earn more than 8x your rate! To do this, estimate the length of time you will need to finish the project; it's easy if you have done the task countless of times before. Multiply that with your INCREASED hourly rate and add a certain percentage (10% or 15%).
- If you are unfamiliar with the task, be honest with your client.
- Don't be greedy; charging per project makes it easy for you to double, triple, or quadruple your earnings, but in doing so, you will risk losing your clients!

Just be honest with yourself: how good are you in what you do? Have you invested money on training? Are you a specialist in your niche?

IMPORTANT: Never underprice your service even at the beginning stage. Doing that will brand you as the clients' "go to VA if they have low budget". Let's say you started at $10 per hour; by the time an increase in rate is necessary, the client may relent, but he will expect you to do more tasks! When that happens, it's as if you didn't increase your rate!

Once a client **probes too much** on your rate, asking why your rates are high and why you are better than others, chances are, he wants you to lower it down. Deflect. That client may be a nightmare in the making.

Making it big in the Virtual Assistants World has great, great benefits; the best of which is this: **clients will come to you**. Instead of writing proposals or sending out bids, you actually work billable hours! You can take projects which suit your taste, ensuring that you won't be bored or stressed. You will never run out of jobs because business owners will seek your service.

I want to help you reach that point, hence, the entire chapter for marketing your business. However, I must tell you that you need several things before you even dream of having a stream of clients on your waiting list.

- A good profile, with great feedback from clients. Whether you work in Upwork, Freelancer, Guru, or Fiverr, you need to have a good standing. If your profile is plagued with "missed deadlines", "disorganized methods", or "lack of communication" comments, no client will come near you.

- Leverage: what makes you special? Are you better equipped? More trained? Have more experience in the niche?

If you have those things, let's get started!

Creating a Website

Websites are very important to a virtual assistant because it serves as the portal where the clients could find him. This is where portfolio and testimonials could easily be viewed and evaluated. It also gives a professional feel, ultimately making your client feel safe in his dealings with you. Below are the guiding steps you can perform in creating your virtual assistant website:

1. Start a WordPress site; Blogger is also good – choose one which exudes comfort. These two gives you the option to blog, which may be useful to promote your business.

2. Buy a domain name – Using WP or Blogger is free, but your website will look like this: www.christinethebestva.wordpress.com or www.christinethebestva.blogspot.com, it's very amateur, so you have to stick to .com. You can buy domain names for as low as $10/year in NameCheap or GoDaddy.

3. Choose a hosting like Bluehost; I suggest for you to use a hosting site that is different from where you got your domain name. Doing this will make it easier for you to transfer in case you decide to move elsewhere.

4. Now, it's time to design and setup your website. If you are not knowledgeable in website creation, might as well ask or pay someone else to do it. Remember: this is business, so the site has to look professional. Things that you may want to include in your website are:

- **Projects you have finished** – be specific with what you did and what you delivered.

- **Testimonials from your clients** – if possible, ask your previous client for their photo and for some comments. These feedbacks will VASTLY help you, so you can't do without them.

- **Your guarantees** – what are your basic guarantees? Beating deadlines, organization, excellent communication skills, and professionalism are just some of them.

- **About You Page** – who are you? When did you start your business? What trainings did you undergo? What's your niche? Explain these things in a professional (but likable) manner so that clients can make an instant connection. Don't forget to have your smiling picture!

- **Contact Page** – Aside from the typical contact page, you may also want to include a separate email address, or Skype ID. You can choose to give your work phone number, too, if you are comfortable.

- **Other Social Media Accounts** – Instantly connect with them using Facebook or Twitter by adding them in your website.

Promoting Your Business

Once a website is created, you need to make it visible to prospective clients by following the steps below:

- Write about 10 articles which you will include in your blog or submit to other websites like Examiner or LifeHacker. The more, the better, but 10 will be a good starting point. Make sure that the articles "subtly" promote you as the best virtual assistant a client can find by making them in first-person perspective and adding touches of your expertise. For example: write about The 10 Qualities a (insert niche here) Virtual Assistant Must Have! IMPORTANT: Don't forget to add some links to your website and blog.

- Hit up relevant Facebook Groups and connect with the members. Join forums, and scout other blogs for the comments section. Never just promote your business; they may label you as a spammer if you do that. Share interesting content (your blog post, for example) and then promote your business website once in a while.

- Traditional promotion like giving out flyers and business cards is still alive, so take advantage of it. Attend commerce events and distribute the flyers and cards to possible clients.

- Write a book which your clients will be interested in; offer it for free in exchange of getting their e-mail addresses. The more e-mail addresses you collect, the more likely it is that you will find clients. Don't forget to send them relevant emails weekly, twice or once a month so that they won't forget you. Also, create an email signature that promotes your business.

- Alternatively, write a book (or several, if you have a knack for it) and sell it on Amazon. Make sure that it is related to your niche. Inside the book, promote your blog and website, as well as your social media accounts.

- Once you are already making money, advertise using Facebook Campaigns or solo ads.

- Make your business more visible online by adding it to Google Places.

While searching about promotions, I found this really helpful article which enumerates the places where you can promote your VA business. Some of the places mentioned are: Longer Days, World Wide 101, Zirtual, and Virtual Assistant Quickstart. Read more here.

Use Blogging to Your Advantage

Earlier, I talked about blogging as a beneficial aspect of promotion. You must be wondering why a very time-consuming activity is so important. I can give you three answers:

- Blogging is YOU TALKING. Reading the post is like having a conversation with you, hence clients will develop a connection.
- Your articles can be forwarded to various places; it can be shared hundreds, perhaps thousands of times. If

that happens, imagine the number of visitors your website will have! The more visitors, the more potential clients!

- It keeps your website updated. Some clients become hesitant when they see a website with no update, so ease their worries by writing blogs even once a week or once every two weeks!

Now, I am not saying that blogging is the heart and soul of promotion, just that they are a big part of it. If you don't want a blog because of personal reasons, no problem. Just make sure that you are visible online.

Let's see. You now have a website, a Facebook page, and even Twitter. Since you saved a portion of your earnings for promotion, there's a steady stream of traffic in your website and social media accounts. One day, you woke up and noticed that you have 4 emails, all are asking for a quote on their project OR they are asking for your hourly rate. How will you respond?

It's NOT smart to say yes to all four; however, it's also not wise to decline those which you seem to dislike. The best approach is to talk to them via phone or Skype so that you can know more about the task. Discuss the following:

- The goal of the job or the things that should be delivered.

- When should the job be completed? Is it short term or long term?
- Is it urgent? This is important in case you can take ALL the projects through prioritizing.
- What's the budget of the client?

After discussing these things, decide if you will take all or just some of the projects offered to you. The criteria will be:

- How you like to do the job
- The amount of time given to you; and
- The rate or the budget*

*In case you like the job, BUT feel like the budget is too low, don't directly tell your client about it! You can't just say *"I'm sorry, but your budget is too low."* You have to make him understand that increasing the rate will also increase the quality of the project. For an instance, if he wants to finish a project in a week's time so he can save up, tell him about the things you need to do and how much time it will take you to do it. Researching and writing, for example, takes time – it shouldn't be rushed.

Whenever requests pour, you have to be honest with your capabilities. If you are still working with one client, say so; don't say yes to requests just because you don't want to lose the chance. I know a lot of people who took more bites than they can chew; in the end, the clients were so dissatisfied that they warned their friends from hiring those VA's.

A steady stream of clients is good; it means that you are building up quite nicely. The technique to keep things that way is to prioritize and maintain the high-quality delivery.

Chapter 7 - Getting Paid

Getting paid is perhaps the best part of being a virtual assistant because finally, you will see the fruits of your labor. Most of the VAs I know use the online website where they were hired as the method of payment. Example: Upwork uses a **Teamwork App** which tracks the time you work. It captures screenshots while you are working so the client can be certain that you are doing your job and not just surfing the net. The only problem here is when the site is down – the app can only cache 4 hours of work, so the rest will not be recorded. At the beginning of the project, discuss the steps you will take when these scenario happen. Once the time has been recorded and reviewed, weekly payment is guaranteed.

Escrow is also popular and convenient for fixed-price assignments. In this method, sites require the clients to fund the project first before the job officially starts. That way, you can work with peace of mind, not worrying whether the client will pay you or not. The funds will be released after the client approves the work. All the online hiring websites we have mentioned use this method.

To get paid, here are the things that you need:

- **A separate checking account**. You need to separate the finances of your business from your personal money, so open another bank account. You can connect this bank account to your chosen platform, OR it can be used separately, especially for contracts you got on your own.

- **PayPal** which is solely for your business. PayPal is widely used by clients because invoices can be sent with ease. You can use PayPal in contracts which you have obtained using your own means, like your website or Facebook Page.

- **A credit card**. To be able to withdraw money from your PayPal account, you need to verify it using a credit card. I know some people who are doubtful to have a credit card for their business; if you are one of them, inquire about "prepaid" credit cards – those which can be loaded. From what I know, PayPal acknowledges them for verification.

For your security, I advise you to do the following:

- When hired on sites like Upwork, Freelancer, or Guru, **use the platform's message board** for updates which concern important things like revisions, additional tasks, change in payment scheme, or increased rate. Major changes should be documented.

- **Secure a legal contract.** You will find that even in online hiring sites, contracts are crucial because they protect you. Contracts will also be your saving grace in times when clients become a nightmare. Just make sure that the documents have the following:

- Your legal names
- Valid addresses and contact numbers
- List of deliverables (if applicable) or the goal of the job
- Your rate
- Starting and ending point of project
- Payment scheme
- Other important things

- **Update the contract** whenever necessary.

- **Keep all the records** and have a backup system. Aside from using tools like Dropbox and Google Docs, purchase a portable hard drive and save all the documents there, including contracts, NDAs, and receipts. I know it is time-consuming, but it's necessary.

- **Read everything at least twice before signing.**

- **Try to get paid weekly.** Working with a new client and not sure if you can trust him despite the binding contract? Tell him (politely) that you will feel more comfortable in getting paid weekly OR by milestones.

- **Invoice in detail.** Whenever sending out an invoice, be very specific with what you did, what you delivered, and if you did extra tasks.

Getting paid is all about documentation, organization, and thinking ahead.

While the best part of being a VA is getting paid, it's getting the feedback that keeps you going. After the job – which means after you got paid – you need to follow up. Things you can tell the client are:

- "Thank you for trusting me, it was a pleasure doing business with you. I know it's not much but I found the following references useful for your business..."
- "Let me know if you encounter any mistakes on what I did/delivered. I checked everything twice, but just in case I missed some things – just send me a message and I'll revise it immediately."
- "I found these additional tasks to be helpful, you can read more about it here. I am knowledgeable in doing these tasks, so if you decide to go on, just send me a message."

- "Here's the summary of what we did. I would like to ask for a little favor; can I get a feedback from you? A short comment would go a long way for my business. If possible, can I have your photo, too? I'll include them in the feedbacks section of my site – I'll send you a link once it's updated."

The rule is to make sure that the client is satisfied – as long as he's not asking you to do tasks that are not included in your job description AND he's not asking you to change things that are not wrong, you should welcome his requests for revision. Giving him pieces of advice and leading him towards other tasks which you can do, will ensure your place as a valuable business contractor.

Before I show you the proper way of handling bad clients, let us first set the boundaries straight: how can a VA say that a client is bad? Below are some of the criteria:

- He doesn't know what he wants. When a client often pussyfoots on his instructions, that's a bad sign. Chances are, he will ask you to do *this*, then demand that you *revise* it and do *that* instead. You'll be overworked and underpaid.

- He pays, but in a late fashion. Worse, he will continually tell you that he will send the payment later, tomorrow, or next week.

- He doesn't communicate as often as needed.

- He asks for a huge discount because it's his first time working with you and he wants to be certain that the two of you will "click" first.

- He is rude. Despite your numerous attempts to make him see that one method is better than the other, he insists – rather impolitely – that he knows more than you do, and that your idea sucks.
- He's a scope creep: always demanding to do things that are not in your contract.

How to deal with these bad clients:

If your experience is bad (late payments, pussyfooting, lack of communication, rude), and you don't want a repeat performance, don't accept another contract from this client BUT do it politely. **Additional Tip:** To avoid late payments, have a "late payment" fee in your contract.

If he's asking for a huge discount, explain that you can't do that because you will be underpaid. Offer a regularly paid trial:

for example, work for a day or two with him and then let him evaluate your performance.

Scope creep? Politely remind him that the job is not in your contract and then give him the additional charge in case he wants to pursue.

Chapter 10 - Furthering Your Career

If you want more clients, you need to expand your skills and knowledge. As mentioned earlier, you can enter Virtual Assistance Training online – there are free courses as well as paid.

You can start with a free course here: http://www.vaclassroom.com/. After the free version, there's a premium for $24 monthly. Too heavy? Try the onetime payment of less than $70 here: https://www.expertrating.com/certifications/Virtual-Assistant-Certification/Virtual-Assistant-Certification.asp

You can also go to **Alison** – a lot of free courses on the use of Excel, PowerPoint, Google Apps, and WordPress are available there. If you are looking for some more structured paid classes, search at **Udemy**.

Help yourself more by reading free blog posts from **Hubspot** and **Copyblogger**. Scout **Amazon Kindle** for free books about virtual assistance. There are many ways to further your career, so don't stagnate.

Conclusion

Congratulations! You are now more equipped to start your Virtual Assistant Business. The next steps you have to do are listed below:

1. Decide on the niche you'll concentrate on. List down all the skills needed for that particular niche. For example: bookkeeping niche needs knowledge in excel; are you skillful enough to proceed? Evaluate yourself and then train on the aspects which you think you are lacking.

2. Think of a good business name and head to your area's business information center to inquire about the permits, licensing, and taxation.

3. Set up your own home office!

4. Start a profile. Choose the secured online hiring website and begin looking for jobs. Don't forget to make your pitches short but remarkable – think: authority and likability. After each job, don't hesitate to ask for a feedback.

5. Already in a good standing? Let's say you've finished about 15 projects, most – if not all – were successful. You can now create your own website and blog, join forums and groups, and interact to promote your business!

Your business will grow – don't make haste but don't be afraid of risks. Be careful in your transactions and NEVER start a project without funds, unless of course, you asked for an upfront OR you trust your client.

I wish all the best for your new business! Cheers!

Take a Leap of Faith and Start a Photography Business

A Beginner's Guide to Starting a Successful Business as a Photographer

Russell Davis

Table of Contents

Introduction

Think of 10 people you know who detest picture-taking? Those who don't want to be included in group pictures and who have not yet taken a single selfie. I doubt you'll be able to name 5, much less 10. This is because everyone wants to keep the good memories alive and the easiest way to do that is to take a picture. Despite the fact that people now own smart phones with great cameras, nothing can beat the skill of a professional photographer – they just know the nuts and bolts of taking photos, editing, and printing. They know about the correct angle, the right amount of light, and even the appropriate gesture and expression. These are just some of the reasons why I'd personally hire a photographer for special events rather than let every guest or participant take their own photos. Photography services are just more organized, more effective, and they give better-looking images that you can proudly post online.

Collectively, this is the reason why a photography business is in demand.

Now, this book will guide you in starting your own business; it's truly an advantage if you are a photographer by profession, but if not, it doesn't mean that you could not open your own business. I can help you get the ball rolling. Here's a peek inside the book:

- The 4 main markets you should choose from in starting a photography business
- A list of the investments you should make, including tips and tricks; this includes camera, lighting, backdrops, etc.
- How do you legalize your business? What about licenses? Permits? Taxes? What is LLC?
- A step-by-step guide on how you can promote your business
- Should you declare copyright on your photos?

- Best printers according to reviewers

- What you need to include when creating a contract

- How will you encourage your clients to leave reviews?

- Analyzing your business and "stalking" your competition

- And a whole lot more!

I know that starting a photography business – any business, in fact – is not a walk in the park. It's also not roses and rainbows; there will be difficulties along the way and maybe at one point you might even think of quitting. Lower your chances of being discouraged by being equipped – one way to do that is to read, savor, and finish this book.

So, if you're all set... let's go!

Chapter 1 - First and Foremost, Cover the Basics

As with any other business, starting means covering the basics first before moving on to the harder parts. In this chapter, we will cover two things: your target market and what you know about that target market. I know you probably want to jump the gun already, but these two are as important as the technicalities which you are excited about.

What is your market?

When we say "market" we are actually referring to the "genre". We have 4 and all of them still have subcategories, so take your time in choosing which you like best. You might already have a genre in mind, but don't skip this chapter; who knows, you might change your decision in the process. Just remember to consider your interest during this genre selection. You don't want to merely choose a market just because it's high-paying, or just because it's easier than the others. On the other side, I am not saying that you should only consider your interest; a mix of every aspect will be your best bet.

First up, we have the **Creative Genre**. From the word itself, you can deduce that the core of this photography is beauty or aesthetics. The photos can be edited using software programs and they can be mass-produced. Subcategories of this genre are:

- Studio photography
- Photos for catalogues
- Fashion
- Taking photos of celebrities
- Advertising (Posters, commercials, etc.)
- Food
- Still Life

- Pornography

Just a quick note: among all the other genres, the Creative Category exercises the most freedom; however, it doesn't mean that it should not be subjected to the accepted laws of photography which states that you should not violate or condemn the existence of the subject – you can only take shots and appreciate that they are present. For an instance, albeit pornography is an accepted subcategory, many people would still find it unethical, especially if you reduce the subjects into mere sources of pleasure instead of appreciating them as human beings.

Then, we have the **Editorial Genre**. Compared to the Creative Category, the rules of this genre is far stricter; you will know why by identifying some of the subcategories:

- Archival

- Architectural

- Those concerning nature, like wildlife, marine, landscape, etc.

- Life, like photojournalism, travel, and documentaries

- Sports

- Scientific Photos

- Corporate purposes

- Military purposes

- Celebrity photos like those taken by paparazzi

- Taking photos in a ramp fashion show

If you can freely blend photos in the Creative Genre, you cannot do so in the Editorial Genre because what you want is to portray the truth – as close to the reality as possible. If there is a need to alter the image, it should be minimal and the only reason would be because you want to showcase the scene more clearly. Although the rules are stricter, it does not mean that this category is more ethical than the Creative market: for an instance, works of paparazzi that invade the homes of celebrities already constitute violation of the right to privacy.

The third is what we call as **Retail Genre**. You are most definitely familiar with this market because you have probably already hired a photographer once for retail purpose. According to Shutha.org, Retail Photography deals with the person on the street who needs a photographer to capture significant achievements as an aid to memory. Examples of these achievements are:

- Weddings
- Birthdays
- Baptismal
- Funeral
- Graduation
- Rite of Passage
- Sports

- Services in a studio (passport size photos, family portraits, ID pictures)

- Sports events

Last but not the least, we have the 4th Genre: **Personal.** This is the category we are most familiar with, after all, we go in our day to day living taking personal photos. You must be asking: can I have a business out of this 4th category? The answer is yes, you definitely can, but you won't be providing the actual service; instead, you can provide the following:

- Your cameras and other equipment

- Your knowledge (you can train people to become photographers)

- The post-processing of photos or even the printing

Another quick note: sometimes, there's a thin line between the Genres; for example: travel photos can be editorial if you want to see what truly happened in the journey, especially if the subject is a known personality; however, you can take travel photos personally (4th genre), alter them and mass produce them, for Creative Purposes.

Now, take the time to pick a genre, and then decide on the subcategory. Be serious, but don't be too hard on yourself. You are just about to start your business, so nothing is set to stone as of now. Again, consider your interest, then think of the demand, your capital, the time you have in your hands, and the available people who can and will help you.

What do you know about that market?

After choosing your market, the next step is for you to evaluate what you already know of your genre. Often times, people who venture in photography business are photographers by profession, but that's not always the case. You should also not be discouraged in case you know nothing about cameras. In other words, look into yourself and see where improvement is needed. To help you, here's a list of questions you can ask yourself:

- How is my skill and knowledge in taking photos in my chosen genre? Contrary to popular belief, it's **not** always a point-and-shoot technique. Depending on the genre, you have to obtain certain skills. If you are lacking in this area, attend seminars or short-courses, read books, and watch videos; little by little, you will have what it takes to supervise your business.

- Is there any competition? If there are, how are they faring? What should my business accomplish in order to have a neck-to-neck battle with them or better yet, be more successful than my competition?

- Can I branch out in the near future? For example, if I opted for studio photography catering to portraits and family photos, I might as well offer ID pictures, or retail photography.

- How much is my capital? What can I obtain using this capital? Please note that while it is a common practice to borrow money to start a business, it is not recommended. I gather that since you pick this book, you probably already have a budget in mind – make the best out of that capital before considering loans.

- What do I know about photography business in general? This book will cover the basics, but it's still wise to have a baseline data.

Now that we've established the possible markets for you, I want you to take the time and research some more. You can proceed to the next chapter as early as now, but it would be beneficial for you

to have the genre first.

Chapter 2 - Get Real on Your Investments

Any business requires an investment; in fact, any business requires several investments. Question: when do we say that an investment is big or small? $10,000 is a really big investment compared to $1,000, so does that mean that we are only talking about finances?

Not really.

You see, as a business owner, you need to invest more than just dough; you need time, effort, and manpower. As for gauging the size of the investment, it depends on several factors:

- What can you easily give? If you have $2,000 lying around – amount which you do not need – then it's just a small investment. However, if $2,000 is what it takes for you to be homeless or hungry, then it certainly would be a big investment.

- Do you still have a day job? If yes, then time will be a huge capital. You'll need to prioritize things, schedule appointments wisely, and have a "close door policy" so that you can think of nothing but your business alone.

- Who'll help you with your business? If your wife/husband or parents are willing to help you, then you can do a lot more without exhausting manpower options (i.e. paying for other people to do the job).

At this point, you have to reflect: how prepared am I? How much is the ready capital that I have? Can I free my weekdays for this business in case I choose to keep a day job? Do I want to do this business alone or will I feel more at ease with a partner?

Now that the hard part is cleared up, we'll now move on to the tangible aspects of investment. Below are the basic things you'll need to start the business; don't forget to list them down (itemize), together with the price (if applicable), so that you will know exactly the amount of money you spent.

Your Business Name

You can't have a business without a name! Think simple, but catchy – something that people will easily relate to photos or captured moments (i.e., Great Image, Candid Shots). If you want your name included in the business, a simple "surname + photography" formula will do; for example: McFarland Photography – this will be very beneficial if your name is already linked to photography.

Business name is important: don't forget that it will appear on the photos, on paper bags, website, business cards, brochures, and catalogues, so choose wisely!

The Best Camera for Your Business

Quality of photos, affordability, and comfort: these are just some of the things which you need to keep in mind when choosing a camera for your genre. I will assume that most of you here are already well-versed with cameras, but I'll still discuss this section briefly in case some of you are just starting out; at least with these criteria covered, you will be equipped when purchasing the camera.

Think of your genre: if you are planning on studio photography business, a bulky camera and accessories might be okay. If you go for photographing special occasions like weddings and birthdays, then consider the portability of the equipment.

Now as for the key settings, you should think of these:

- ISO

- Aperture

- Shutter speed

ISO (which is not an acronym) is the sensitivity of the camera's sensor to light. Most cameras operate at ISO 1000, and that's good, but even better if you have cameras that naturally operate at a higher level, like NIKON'S D4 and CANON'S 5D MARK III which have ISO 12,800. Please note that most digital cameras can adjust the ISO level, but it can also alter the quality of the image, making it look unnatural.

The next key setting you have to give attention to is **Aperture**.

Aperture is the f-number you see when you look at the features of the camera. It may look and sound confusing, but this feature is very basic. Say for example you need more light, then what you'll do is adjust the diameter of your camera's lens, pulling it as far back as possible. If you need less light, then you have to narrow the hole of the opening. Hence, aperture is simply the measure of lens opening's diameter.   The smaller the f-number, the wider the diameter, meaning more light will enter. Remember this: more is not always good because your camera may capture unnecessary light that your image does not need.

Frankly speaking, this feature can be adjusted and most modern cameras will make a suggestion as to what scale should be used; my advice is for you to make sure that your camera has that suggestion feature.

Last of the features we will discuss is the **Shutter Speed**. This setting dictates how long the shutter will remain open; it is measured in just fractions of one second, hence if you see a shutter speed of 1/125, it means that the shutter will remain open for only 125th of a second. The higher the number, the less the time the shutter is open, the sharper the image. If your camera has lower shutter speed (1/6, for example), your photos might turn out blurry, but you can remedy that by using equipment like tripod.

Again, most cameras have an auto-adjustment feature, but if you're wondering about the best shutter speed for a certain shot, you can refer to this article.

Now, for the costs: a quick look at Amazon and you'll learn that most digital cameras come from $185-$500 price range; others can go as high as $1000+.

Lighting

Lighting is crucial for good-quality photos, especially if your business is studio photography or if you'll take photos at night. Softbox Lighting Kit can be bought at $75 while the Continuous Lighting Umbrella Kit can be purchased at $27 to $55.

Backdrops and Accessories

Backdrops or backgrounds are important if you will have a studio photography business. For ID photos, a white (or plain) background is most essential; you can buy 100% muslin cloths (5 ft. by 7 ft.) for only $16, but don't forget that you also need a stand for that ($35). For portrait photos, various designs are available; their prices vary depending on size, material, and of course, design.

Photobooth services also require backdrops, but instead of using muslin cloths, most owners use tarpaulin sheets which have designs appropriate to the celebration.

Digital Props

Costumes, cute things like pirate hats, and even the big mug where some photographers place a smiling baby – yes, these are all under the Digital Props Category. To be honest, it could be anything from under the sun! To make it easier for you, shop for them in bulk and categorize them per season or occasion, like birthdays, wedding, graduation, baptism, Valentine's Day, etc. Another way to shop for them is to have themes ready: for example, a vintage theme requires old-looking objects, a summer theme probably needs picnic baskets, wide hats, and beach props.

The key here is to keep your genre in mind: if you will venture on portrait photography or photobooth service, then you WILL NEED A LOT of these digital props; a wedding photography business (especially prenup shoots) on the other hand needs less since most of the time, the future wife and groom will contribute on the costumes and props. Now, if your business only caters to ID pictures, photographing events like sports, graduation, or baptism ON THE SPOT, then you have no need for these props because you want to capture the moments as they are.

Your Studio or Office

Perhaps the most difficult and complicated portion of building a photography business is setting up your "headquarters". Desiring a portrait photography business means you need to find a place, buy it, or rent it – whatever works for you. Of course, owning it has the advantage of not paying the rent, but in case you don't have the dough to buy space yet, you can rent a small room or office and make the most of it. Don't let not having your own place stop you from starting your business.

Choose your location wisely: ID or class pictures will do especially well if your studio is near academes, schools, or universities. Portrait Business? You might want to consider a stall in a local mall or a place which families often visit.

For photobooth services, you don't need a studio – one advantage you'll love. You just need a reliable website (a Facebook Page will even do!), and several contact numbers where possible clients can reach you.

What if my business is about photographing events or occasions? Do I need a studio? No. You just need your camera, your computer (with editing software, preferably), and your printer – but always,

always make sure that you have a spare of everything just in case one malfunctions.

Hey, how about still life photography? Is a studio needed? Yes. But the studio does not need to be expensive; in fact, you can have one at home! Just purchase several rolls of white paper (or paint a room white, if you can) and secure them in place using duct tapes or clamps. A 48" by 200ft roll costs about $20. Have some foldable tables ready, and set up your lighting equipment as well as your tripod. Kristen Leighty showed her skills in making an inexpensive studio here.

Note: the techniques to have your own studio at home is also applicable for ID pictures business and portrait photography; just watch this video as a guide. You know what that means, right? Less expenses!

Photo-editing Software

Not all businesses require "raw" photos; in fact, a lot of clients now appreciate if their images are made sharper and clearer, that's why we included it in your investments list. Your first choice would probably be Adobe Photoshop, and that's a wise choice seeing that Adobe already has a good reputation; however, don't forget that there are others like: Serif Affinity Photo, PhaseOne Capture One Pro9, Corel PaintShop Pro X8, ON1 Photo 10, and Cyberlink PhotoDirector 6 Ultra.

Editorial Photography businesses need less of this software; to be honest, it's better to use them as seldom as possible – in doing so, you will establish your business as one that provides "natural" shots. The technique here is to gauge the beauty of the scene first before you hit the button and then take multiple shots of the scene. Oh, and don't forget to invest on extra SD cards.

How many people are needed to get your business rolling? Freelance photographers often need no one but themselves, but sometimes, assistants are also necessary. For portrait photography, you need someone to man the desk or the cashier; the photographer, aside from taking photos, also does the editing and the cutting of pictures. Photobooths need at least 2 people: one mans the digital camera, the other does the lay outing/editing and printing. A business that takes wedding or birthday photos need at least three people for the event.

In starting a business, it is important to hire only those whom you will need.

These investments are necessary, but then again, I don't know the exact genre you have in mind, so the last say is still yours. Shop for only those things that you need, ask questions, scout the area for better finds – just don't procrastinate. You can start your business at a small scale level and then just work it up.

Chapter 3 - Legalize Everything

Licensing

Is your photography business coming along just fine? I have good news for you: most jurisdictions in the United States require no licensing for your photography business as reported by Improve Photography. However, there are exceptions to this unspoken rule, so for your peace of mind and to ensure that your business is in the map, make two phone calls: a) to the State Licensing Board, and b) to the City Hall. The people in these departments will notify you if licensing is no longer necessary; if it is, they will instruct you on what to do.

Taxes

Most jurisdictions will require you to pay **sales tax** because they deem your business as selling a product instead of giving a service. The process of obtaining a certificate is actually short, but you may want to consult an accountant on the actual process of paying the taxes.

Business Permit

Now, as for the business permit, you don't have to worry about paying a dime, except of course for your gasoline or your transportation fees and some photocopies they will require of you. The permit will be released in 2-3 days; call your county and your city and ask for the process. The government knows that a business is good for the area, so the process will not be stressful.

Obtaining an LLC

Limited Liability Company or LLC is one of the ways by which you can be protected against SOME lawsuits. Examples of how it can protect you are below:

- In case of force majeure situations where in you were not able to do as your contract says, the client cannot collect your personal assets.
- If ever you gave ugly photos which the clients hate, they cannot sue you personally, BUT they can sue your business.

In other words, LLC is used to separate you and your personal assets to your business. Still, keep in mind that it WON'T protect you from everything; you shouldn't treat it as an immunity against charges. For example: if you forgot to pay your sales taxes, the IRS will be able to get your personal assets – the LLC won't stop them.

The advice is for you to obtain LLC if:

- You have personal assets you want to protect, like a house, car, bank accounts, boats, etc.

- You expect to earn a lot in your business ($80,000 or more)

- You will take pictures of celebrities (you know how they love to sue)

- You intend to venture in commercial photography

- You want to have peace of mind

If, however, you only want to take photos part time, or if you have no bank accounts or assets to protect, LLC might not be necessary.

Chapter 4 - Step by Step Guide on How to Promote Your Business

Our era today makes almost everything easy, what with the digital invasion that took place. Of course, you can use online techniques to promote your business, but the question is: how? Below is the step by step guide.

1. Start a Facebook Page – If you can't have a website just yet, you should definitely create a Facebook page. Don't forget to upload your previous works, as clients often judge them and use them as a guide on whether they will contact you or not. Don't forget to include the name of your business in the pictures themselves, so that no matter how many times they are shared, your brand is still visible.

2. Have a blog – Yes, I know it's time consuming, but doing this will let Google know that your business is there. Remember to use related keywords and to share your blog links in various social networking sites like Twitter, Instagram, Facebook, and Pinterest. Another good advantage of having a blog is it works like a website: you can have pages where your work can be displayed and where you can give your services in detail.

3. Scout other blogs, website, and Facebook Groups – Contribute to those sites to establish yourself as an authority. After saying something relevant, share you works or your blog content.

4. Explain your packages in detail, but also let them know if you accept custom services – Remember this: when a client goes to your website or Facebook page, he or she would be interested to know what's included in your services, especially the price and rates.

5. Have discounts, promos, or bonuses, especially on your business' opening or anniversary – Let's be honest, people love discounts, promos, and bonuses, so take advantage of it. To make it more profitable for your business, give these advantages by announcing online contests, where participants will have to Like and Share your post.

6. Seize the opportunities at events – If you happen to be shooting events, like birthdays and weddings, seize the opportunity to give out flyers or business cards! You might not know it, but one or few of the guests will also have parties of their own in the future – if they liked your photos, they will definitely keep you in mind.

Pro Tip: Pick photos (preferably some which the client didn't choose), upload them on Facebook, and tag your clients. This is a good strategy, since when the photos are shared, your Facebook page will appear and other people can click it.

7. Word of mouth still works – just because we are in the digital era doesn't mean that word of mouth promotion no longer works. Personal referrals from your previous clients are powerful. How do you encourage them to spread the positive review? Simple: you have to do a great job.

Pro Tip: Remind them to recommend you to their friends by sending out a Thank You Card after each successful project.

8. And finally, have a portfolio website – Once you have collected significant amount of photos from projects, upload them as a part of your portfolio in your website. Of course, don't forget to also upload them in Facebook, Pinterest, or Instagram – whatever social media you have.

I know about your worries: a) having a website is expensive, b) it demands time, and c) it would be hard if you know nothing about website creation and design. I recommend trading for you – find someone who is willing to create your portfolio website in exchange for your service as a photographer. You can also start out free using platforms like Wix, Weebly, or WordPress. These sites have portfolio templates in them – all you need to do is drag and drop the elements.

Whatever strategies you include, don't forget to concentrate on your target market. It wouldn't do you well to bombard the wrong people with advertisements – you risk annoying them and they might give bad reviews instead of spreading how good your business is.

Chapter 5 - What to do after getting a client?

Once the business is in the zone, clients will start calling you and some of them (if not, hopefully all) will choose you to cover their event. At this point you will feel like you are on top of the world, but don't be complacent! Sure, you have to give it your best so that the client will be happy and give you great reviews, but there are other things you have to keep in mind. Those critical points are listed below:

Contracts - What's included?

As a professional, it's always (as in, always) safe to have a contract that will protect you and your business against abusive clients or clients who have no intention to pay in full. Once you have secured a client, talk to him or her and draw up the terms which are acceptable to the both of you. The most critical of these terms are as follows:

- **Basic information** like full name, address, contact information of BOTH parties
- **Exact number of hours of work** – please state clearly when the work will begin and at what time, and when it will end and at what time. Believe me when I say that it will save you someday – some clients will take advantage of your service, especially at events that last all night long. If you don't have a firm timeframe in your contract, the typical 8-hour gig may turn into 12-14 hours! And guess what? Because those hours in excess are not included in your contract, you won't get paid for them unless the client develops the decency to do so!
- **The price and rates** – do you wish to be paid per hour, or do you have a flat rate charge? Most photographers combine these two: having a flat rate charge and then charging per

hour if the project extends. Be very specific with what's included in those price or rates and always include scenarios in which the client will demand more aside from what's already in the package.

- **Methods and terms of payment** – how and when will the client pay you? What happens in the event that he or she pays late or worse, fails to pay? If a deposit is required, state so and give a definite due date. Same with the payment – have a date ready and let the client know that the date is ironclad by giving fees for late payment.

- **Deliverables** – If you didn't already mention what's included in the Price and Rate section, the Deliverables section should cover each item that you are supposed to give to the client. Having packages is an advantage, since they are well-structured and specific, but in case the client wants more, then enumerate them in this section. Also, don't fail to include the date of the delivery and what will happen should you fail to deliver in time or if you fail to deliver at all.

- **Long-Term Rights** – How can the client use your photos? Will you allow them to use it commercially? If so, are there added fees? What can they do with it? Can they upload it on Facebook and other Social Media Networks? If so, do you think having your business' watermark in each provided photo is wise? Be specific about your rights and the client's rights once the photos are handed out to them.

Copyrighting Your Work

Let me first say that your photos' copyright remains yours unless you die or you give it away. In fact, you don't need to declare anything since a Copyright is "automatic" – as soon as you have clicked the button, the right is yours. Photos for weddings, birthdays, and other events typically pose no problem as they are mainly used personally; still though, should the client upload the images and turn them into stock photography, or worse, use them obscenely, you will be placed on a hot seat. That's why it is important to list down what the clients can and cannot do once the photos are given to them in either print or digital formats.

Another way to enforce your right is to give out pictures with watermarks in them. The mark should be small, but visible and it should clearly have your name or the name of your business in it. In case you are in the US and want a more in depth way of securing your rights, you can go here and register your photo.

Pricing Your Photography

This section is a bit personal, so I would be quick: pricing your photography totally depends on you. But of course, I will not leave you high and dry; I'll give you the following reminders:

- How much is your hourly rate? Please consider this even if you want to have fixed-priced projects and services.

- How difficult will the job be for you?

- Understand that what you bill isn't what you earn – you have travel expenses and printing expenditures. Being self-employed also means you won't have corporate pension and you won't have paid vacation leaves.

- Depending on your business, you may not have a steady stream of clients.

Keep all these in mind when pricing not just your photography, but also your service.

Printing Your Photos

Printing your photos is a vital part of business; the quality of image is not only affected by how you took the photo, but also by how and where you printed it. According to TopTen Reviews, the best photoprinter is HP PhotoSmart C310A, which costs around $130. Another excellent printer is HP Photosmart D110A, which is far more expensive: $399. Now, once you have chosen your printer, ask the salesperson or research for the best photo paper for that printer.

Chapter 6 - After the Job

Once the deliverables have been sent and the clients finished the payment, what will you do? Earlier, we discussed about sending them a Thank You Card, but you shouldn't stop there! If the client has been especially easy to work with, as in he didn't demand anything other than what's included in the package he purchased, you can give him bonus framed photos or even extra wallet-sized prints. Other than those, you can also:

Send a Reminder Card along with the Thank You Card

The Reminder Card talks about what they can and cannot do with the photos; to make it "friendlier" and so that you won't appear as someone who couldn't trust them, you can include tips and hacks in taking good cellphone pictures. This is also a good way to remind them that you might use their photos as a part of your portfolio.

Tell them that the images may appear not just in your website, but also in your social media accounts as well as in your studio.

Ask them for feedback

Politely asking clients for their feedback is a good way to improve your business: they tend to be honest, so you will know exactly where you need to get better at. The easiest way to do this is to verbally ask them; however, it might turn awkward with clients who don't do well in giving negative remarks face to face. The best way is to give them a form in print or online. The areas you should cover are: quality of service, quality of photos, ease of transaction, and price. You should also give them room for personal comments. At the end of the feedback form, remind them that their review may be published on your website, together with their name, date of the event, package they chose, and some of their photos.

Encourage Them to Recommend Your Business to Friends and Family

Okay, tread carefully here because you don't want to be redundant. I'm not telling you to talk to them directly and ask to be recommended – your great work will do that for you. What you'll do is collect their email address and ask them to be a part of your list. Mention that they will receive free newsletters, updates, or tips. You will also send out discounts and bonuses for special occasions. Sending out these emails even just once a month will remind them of you, hence, if a friend of theirs or a family member needs a photographer, your client will probably think of your name first. Alternatively, you can befriend them on Facebook or ask them to like your page, that way whenever you post something, they will remember you.

A business is useless unless you make a profit. Sure, you can say that it was fun, and you made a lot of people happy with the service and photos you have provided them with, but fun alone won't pay the bills, and it certainly won't keep your business from collapsing. More than just earning money, you also need find ways to improve, and you must separate your business with your personal finances.

Separating Your Finances

The first thing you need to do to determine whether you have already made a profit is to separate your personal finances from your business finances. To easily to do this, 2 or more bank accounts may be necessary. The concept is quite simple, but overtime, you may find it taxing; don't relent – this separation is necessary. Below are some of the techniques you can use:

- A box for your business receipts – How do you know what expenses are for your business? Simple: have a separate box where you can keep the receipts related to it.

- A credit card for your business – If you are a credit card person, chances are your finances are already mixed and combined. And I can't blame you! It's really hard to separate your business and personal expenses while using just one credit card! The solution is this: get a separate credit card for your business; not only will this segregate expenditure, it will also build your business credit.

- Business Owner with a salary – Yes, you read that right! Instead of withdrawing all your profits at once, why not just give yourself a monthly salary by taking out a fixed amount of money from the profits? It may sound too restrictive, but in the long run, it will benefit you. I suggest you withdraw most of your earnings in a yearly basis.

- Your business should also have a budget – Just because you see the money on your business side pile up doesn't mean that you can spend as you please! Remember, you don't just want a salary, you want a profitable business that can sustain not just the necessities, but also the luxuries!

The Profit

I would just like to expound on the profits part a bit more. Like I said, it will be helpful to just withdraw a certain amount of money as your monthly salary instead of withdrawing money each time a profit has been made. Let's say you made $4,000 in profits for the month of January - don't withdraw them all! Instead take $2,000 or $2,500 and leave the rest in the business checking account. At the end of the year, if the trend continues like that without a problem, you'll have $18,000 - $24,000!

Is it alright to "stalk" my competition? Of course! It's a given actually, since keeping tabs of your competition is actually a part of your analysis: to see whether you are doing well, or you are being left behind. The only rule is this: NEVER START A GOSSIP that may ruin the reputation of your competitor. At one glance, it seems logical, but in reality, it is unprofessional and uncalled for. Even if the gossip is true, you don't need to spread it – you just have to do better than them.

Start with their website: how do their photos look? What do their clients say about them? Can you get hold of their rates or package prices? Do they have promos which you can modify as your own? Compare these aspects with your business and see the difference.

Instead of "stalking" just one competing business, why not analyze

several? That way, you'll gather more information.

Conclusion

I hope you found all the seven chapters enlightening. I am not going to pretend that this book contains everything you need to know about opening up your own photography business, but I can say with conviction that we've pretty much covered the basics. So... what's next?

First, you have to make a decision: what's your genre going to be? Is it Editorial? Retail? Creative? Or Personal? Most of you will immediately think of Studio Photography concentrating on portraits; if not that, then you will probably select taking photos at events and gatherings. But don't restrict yourself on those choices! If you are happy with freelancing your service, then just improve it – freelancing is also a business, so don't put yourself down.

Next, you have to acknowledge that there is more to learn even though you already are a professional photographer. You have to think business, not just pictures. If you are not a photographer and are just thinking of hiring professionals, I still suggest you study a bit about photography so as to properly supervise your men. Learn from them, too.

Don't forget to itemize all the things you will buy for your business, otherwise, how will you know the exact amount of money you've shelled out? Separation of personal finances from business finances is also important, so prepare a different checking account and credit card. Many photographers who have their own business recommend talking to an accountant about this separation.

Make everything legal – you don't want to start a business, build it up, and then have it crashed because you failed to arrange all the pertinent permits or papers. Consider taxes, licenses, permits, and of course, LLC.

Persevere in finding your clients and once they trust you, do a great job. They will be your best springboard to gain more projects in the future. Don't forget your contract – it's one of the best ways to protect yourself in case lawsuits come your way.

In the end, your experience – both good and bad – will still be the best teacher. Jot down notes, try new tricks, take calculated risks, and ask others for help. Take the whole ordeal seriously, but still enjoy every minute of starting your own business; after all, what good would a business be if it will only cause you stress, heartaches, and frustration?

So to conclude this book, I would like to say thank you for trusting me and congratulations – you have taken the first crucial steps to start a business; don't stop here. Finally, if you have enjoyed this book, I would deeply appreciate if you'll leave a review. It would help me write better books in the future.

www.ingramcontent.com/pod-product-compliance
Lightning Source LLC
Chambersburg PA
CBHW070302190526
45169CB00001B/501